Prayers for My Dear Friend

Hope Lyda

Artwork by
Annie LaPoint

HARVEST HOUSE PUBLISHERS

EUGENE, OREGON

Prayers for My Dear Friend

Text copyright © 2012 by Hope Lyda
Artwork copyright © by Annie LaPoint

Published by Harvest House Publishers
Eugene, Oregon 97402
www.harvesthousepublishers.com

ISBN 978-0-7369-3844-0

All artwork is copyrighted by Annie LaPoint. License granted by Penny Lane Publishing, Inc.®. For more information regarding artwork featured in this book, please contact Penny Lane Publishing at info@pennylanepublishing.com.

Design and production by Garborg Design Works, Savage, Minnesota

Harvest House Publishers has made every effort to trace the ownership of all poems and quotes. In the event of a question arising from the use of a poem or quote, we regret any error made and will be pleased to make the necessary correction in future editions of this book.

Printed in China

12 13 14 15 16 17 18 / FC / 10 9 8 7 6 5 4 3 2 1

To our special new friends Tricia and Noela, who demonstrate the beauty and grace of entrusting a dear friend to god's presence, care, and love.

—Hope and Annie

In all my prayers for all of you,
I always pray with joy...

PHILIPPIANS 1:4

Contents

Prayer, if not the very gate of heaven, is the key to let us into its holiness and joys.

THOMAS BROOKS

There is one friend in the life of each of us who seems not a separate person, however dear and beloved, but an expansion, an interpretation, of one's self, the very meaning of one's soul.

EDITH WHARTON

This is the day the Lord has made; We will rejoice and be glad in it.

Psalm 118:24

belief and beginnings

Dear friend,

I am in awe of your courage as you face a new beginning. You are not alone when you turn toward the unfamiliar horizon, take a step forward, and believe in God's leading. Trust that still small voice guiding you onward. Let go of anything in the past that weighs you down with fear or intimidation. Take a deep breath. Embrace the excitement and anticipation of a fresh start. I cannot wait to see all that God has for you.

For each new morning with its light,
For rest and shelter of the night,
For health and food,
For love and friends,
For everything Thy goodness sends.

RALPH WALDO EMERSON

Life's a voyage that's homeward bound.

HERMAN MELVILLE

god,

Give my friend the courage to move forward with a sense of Your leading. I see her eyes light up with excitement as she talks of this new beginning. May she be given what she needs each step of the way.

Dear friend, you are the most adored flower in the garden of my life.

Lord,

Thank You for providing us with the opportunity to live life with a clean slate. Your mercy covers us as we strive to let go of what is done, so that we can embrace what is yet to be. Show my friend that You are carving out the way for her. Give her eyes that take in the beauty of renewal and a heart that understands the days of her life are in Your care—always have been and always will be.

Creator,

You are the God of sweet surprises. You carve streams in the desert and dreams in the parched land of our doubts. Give my friend the refreshment of such a surprise. May her season of uncertainty flow into a time of abundance, creativity, and renewal.

Psalms 19:8

Kind hearts are the gardens
Kind thoughts are the roots,
Kind words are the flowers,
Kind deeds are the fruits.

Take care of the gardens,
And keep them from the weeds.
Fill, fill them with flowers,
Kind words and kind deeds.

HENRY WADSWORTH LONGFELLOW

Dear friend, savor the sweetness of a new beginning today.

Restorer,

My God, You are so loving and faithful. I pray for Your kiss of restoration to grace the soul of my friend. She needs to believe in beginnings again. She is far enough into her life's journey that she wonders if she has used up her chances to start anew.

Writer of life,

"In the beginning" is the phrase that leads us to the heart and splendor of Your Word. This introduction reminds me that You are the writer of the words and the way to our individual purpose and meaning. Give my friend a heart to understand and ears to hear the words You speak just for her in this time. Lord, let her walk forward with faith in this new life story.

 amen

peace and provision

Dear Friend,

I'm grateful that you remind me of divine faithfulness, which fuels and follows belief and trust in God's provision. Too often I focus so much on my needs that I lose sight of the many incredible ways God provides for us, His daughters. May we embrace the life of peace by remembering to lift up each of our cares, wants, losses, and dreams to the Creator.

Today, I pray that you and I will view every provision, need, and opportunity as a gift from a loving God who replaces every lack with the abundance of peace.

But let all who take refuge in you be glad;
let them ever sing for joy.
Spread your protection over them,
that those who love your name may
rejoice in you.
PSALM 5:11

Friendship improves happiness, and abates misery, by doubling our joy, and dividing our grief.
JOSEPH ADDISON

Dear friend, your faithfulness reminds me of God's goodness.

Lord,

I have watched You clear my friend's heart, life, and path, so that she can walk into purpose with purpose. Long-forgotten ideas, decisions, and moments of faithfulness on her end are now forming a roadway that is solid in Your promises. Give my friend an awareness of all the gifts You have shaped for her and how You are forming in her the great treasure of a fulfilled, beautiful, and purposed woman.

Provider,

My friend needs reminders of Your provision as she waits for a new opportunity. Her heart grows restless as time goes by and the next step remains uncertain. Give her a vision and a hope to hold onto. When she wants to give up, remind her that You've been with her at each turn, in each valley, and through every trial. Let those recollections be a stronger force than any self-doubt that arises.

Psalms 8:1

Lord,

Thank You for listening to the spoken and unspoken prayers of my friend. Allow her to know Your peace intimately, so that she is covered by it as soon as she rises in the morning and filled with it as she lays down to sleep at night.

god,

We view our lives as puzzles with so many oddly shaped pieces and more than a few gaps to fill. You see each life as a whole picture. I lift up my friend today and ask for Your wholeness to be apparent to her. Let her breathe easy and with assurance knowing that those missing pieces are opportunities for Your purpose to complete the picture.

When my friend is weary, Lord, please send the provision of Your supernatural strength. When my friend is anxious, grant her the soothing calm of Your presence. When my friend searches for reasons to keep believing in goodness, bring to her mind the many treasures she's received from Your hand and held in her own hands and heart through the years. When my friend needs a listening ear and a joyful word, let me be the friend she deserves.

 amen

hope and healing

Dear friend,

I believe such blessings of hope and healing are ahead. I know that you've had times of heartache and loss. You face life's trials with an admirable willingness to press on. I love that about you. But I know that the daily burdens and those of larger life weigh you down. I hope that you feel the comfort of companionship as I lift you up and ask God's healing hand, sweet mercy, and saving grace to ease your path today and in the future.

When your tears fall, I want to make it all better. You do the same for me. Just imagine how eager God is to ease our suffering and to guide our steps toward restoration and joy.

A little word in kindness spoken,
a motion, or a tear,
has often healed the heart that's broken
and made a friend sincere.

JOHN GREENLEAF WHITTIER

God,

There can be restlessness in the times of waiting and watching for transformation and renewal. Please ease my friend's worry, so that she can nestle into the assurances of Your loving presence. Your healing goes beyond our desire for immediate rescue, Lord. You stir within my friend a longing for all that is good, righteous, and holy. When she wants to rush the process or step away from the path of healing, may she be given the balm of peace, so that she can bear witness to the miracle of wholeness.

There is no circumstance, no trouble, no testing, that can ever touch me until, first of all, it has gone past God and past Christ, right through to me. If it has come that far, it has come with a great purpose...

ALAN REDPATH

Healer,

I can't see the wounds and scars my friend has hidden from view, but You see the places within...the places that need mending. Thank You for giving us the privilege to pray for one another and to ask for Your healing touch. I lift up my friend and entrust her safety, wisdom, and her every need and hope to Your care.

Dear friend,
the thought of you today
made me smile.

Giver of hope,

When my friend struggles
to recall the melody of hope,
please let her soul tune in to the
harmonies of Your love and grace.
Fill her being—her every cell—
with the warmth and beauty of
lilting delights and choruses of
cheer. Let her prayers be a hymn
of praise to Your ears. As she
awakens, ready to face a new day,
let her soul be flooded with the
gift of a new song.

Every
New Day
is a Gift

god,

I can think of no greater refuge than the shelter of Your affection. I want my friend to experience the healing and ease of coming to You with each and every need. Relationship with You means that she never has to be alone in sorrow or pain or in dire circumstances. You are always with her. I love that Your hope and mercy flood our senses when our frail human hearts grieve and our fragile human bodies break. In this rush of compassion, we are carried to healing.

Lord,

Today I ask You to give my friend the experience of relief in her situation. Let there be a physical sensation of a burden lifted and a wound sealed forever. She has grown weary, and I long for her to have solid rest and peace of mind. Even though she has faith, she carries with her the borrowed doubts of others who speak uncertainty into her life. Release her from the "what ifs" that take over her thoughts, so that she can focus only on Your promises and light.

amen

Our prayer and God's mercy are like two buckets in a well;
while the one ascends, the other descends.

MARK HOPKINS

grace and giving

Dear friend,

I should pay you for an admission ticket! I get a front-row view of your life, and I'm in awe. You juggle responsibilities with flair, carry a basket of tasks on your head, balance a child or a new venture on your hip, dish up servings of kindness for strangers, and offer forgiveness to friends (I know this firsthand). And you do all of this because you care. Deeply. And I adore you for that.

But I've seen your face fall when one piece in your balancing act tumbles out of reach. And I've witnessed you being harder on yourself than you'd ever be to a friend who had a bad day. I pray that God showers you with the grace that you show everyone else. I would be content to watch your heart in action all day…except you inspire me to get out in the world and live like a person who has received grace from the ultimate Giver. Thank you.

And God is able to bless you abundantly, so that in all things at all times, having all that you need, you will abound in every good work.

2 CORINTHIANS 9:8

Dear friend, my last great laugh

Gracious God,

Give my dear friend a great surprise today.
Let her experience a happiness, a delight
she has not felt in years. I pray that each
day a new hope will unfold for her and
help her feel loved and prized. May she
feel showered with grace and goodness
as only You can provide. Let her discover
renewed balance and joy as she pursues
endeavors, dreams, and purpose in You.

Giver of life,

Wholeness can feel unattainable. My friend often examines her wounds
and errors with such scrutiny that she sees them as insurmountable barriers
to a full life. Please give her Your view of those mistakes or hurts. Let her
know in her heart of hearts that each of those wounds was and is a chance to
receive the mending touch of the Savior. Each demonstration of fragility was
and is an invitation to the beauty and fullness of wholeness in You.

was with you! You make joy a reality.

Shepherd,

You lead us and provide for us with such compassion and care. Show my friend that she is one of Your very own. I know there are times when she feels lost and wonders if anyone cares which direction she takes. But I know You hold her life in the palm of Your hand and You breathe hope into her life. Thank You for being the Shepherd who cares deeply for each and every one of Your sheep. When we wander, You search the valleys and the peaks until You find us. You set us free from our self-made traps. And with great tenderness, You bring us home.

Dear friend, let go of anything in the way today... and embrace your unique purpose.

Happiness is as a butterfly, which, when pursued, is always beyond our grasp, but which, if you will sit down quietly, may alight upon you.

NATHANIEL HAWTHORNE

god,

My friend releases others from any sense of judgment or disappointment. She does this because she believes beyond a doubt that You are a God of great grace. Today I ask that my friend consider herself worthy of that grace. May her heart embrace and experience Your mercy, so that redemption becomes a part of her faith story. Thank You for knowing just what my friend needs and for being the Designer of the changed heart.

Lord,

I want the best for my friend. But there are times when I have no idea what that "best" is. There are concerns in her life that she faces with mixed emotions and a divided mind. I don't have the answers. However, when we cannot see beyond today's questions or longings, I can get down on my knees and whisper her name, and You know all there is to know about her. You see what was, what is, and what will be. I pray that she will be guided in Your truth and be nudged toward the very best You have for her.

amen

You make known to me the path of life;
you will fill me with joy in your presence.

PSALM 16:11

purpose and passion

Dear friend,

You are made for so much. There is a spirit of great passion within you that fuels your endeavors and your dreams. And behind that spirit is the Holy Spirit, guiding and discerning so that your steps fall upon the path of purpose God has for you. There is plenty that He wants you to discover and savor in this season. Each change, redirection, and even those down times that appear to be setbacks are parts of the process.

I pray that you will experience the patience and desire to rest in the Spirit's leading. It will awaken your body, mind, and heart to the great, meaningful actions and choices that form your amazing life.

Be glad of life because it gives you the chance to love, to work, to play, and to look up at the stars.

HENRY VAN DYKE

Lord,

Grant my friend the vision to see beyond the temporary obstacles to the vast land of possibility with a path that continues over the hill and around the bend. Your faithfulness is so evident in her life, and she finds comfort in Your never-fading care. Help her to feel confirmation as she prays for and waits on Your guidance.

God,

Reveal to my friend how amazing she is. Let me be one of the voices that cheer for her and speak to her heart with pure truths rather than earthly comparisons that fall short. Give this special woman an understanding of her unique ability. She is the only one You guide toward her special, made-by-Your-hand future. Nobody else could fill those shoes or that purpose.

Dear friend, our prayers for one another connect us to each other and to God's heart.

Provider,

Give my friend a sensitivity to the direction You offer each day. Let her gladly and eagerly set aside worries that plague her thinking and often give force to waves of restlessness. Not only do You hear her prayers and give her the desires of her heart, but You beautifully, tenderly shape those desires as she matures in faith. I see the excitement in her eyes as she discovers new ways to live in Your purpose and live out an existence of meaning.

Lovely flowers are the smiles of god's goodness.

WILLIAM WILBERFORCE

Lover of our souls,

Today I praise You for forming in each of Your daughters a desire and reason to come to You with vulnerability and longing for significance, value, and a true hunger for life. I love my friend. Thank You for kindred spirits in this lifetime. I pray that we make You proud by following Your will and sending along treasures to be found on heaven's shore.

God,
There is so much fire and excitement
that bursts forth when ideas and
plans are aligned with and born of
Your will. Success in the world
can always be used for good.
But when You have planted the
seeds, tended to the
garden of our hopes,
and guided our hearts
to harvest a pursuit
at just the right time, this is
when beauty and dimension
flesh out our dreams. I pray
that my friend has a great season
of harvest and celebration coming
her way. May we praise You for Your
faithfulness in all things.

amen

courage and confidence

Dear friend,

I know you are nervous because there is no turning back. Circumstances have created a distance between what was and what will be. You are on that bridge between. It sways when doubts breeze by, and it seems to lengthen each time something doesn't quite go as planned. But I know who made this bridge and the canyon below.

God says for you to walk this way, to trust His reasons, and to find your footing in His promises. I am cheering you on, friend. I've crossed bridges before, but not this one. This is the one that connects you to your own future. Already I am excited about the moment when you make it to the unshakable ground of God's will. It's right up ahead…and the view is spectacular.

Be absolutely certain that our Lord loves you, devotedly and individually, loves you just as you are… Accustom yourself to the wonderful thought that God loves you with a tenderness, a generosity, and an intimacy that surpasses all your dreams.

ABBÉ HENRI DE TOURVILLE

So do not fear, for I am with you;
do not be dismayed, for I am your god.
I will strengthen you and help you;
I will uphold you with my righteous right hand.

ISAIAH 41:10

god,

I pray that my friend has a strong sense of Your presence today. May she know, without a doubt, that You are holding her hand and gently directing her steps. You speak to her heart directly and let her know of the unfolding promises she can anticipate with peace. Reassure her that Your promises are not just for the future but are also to be experienced right now—they blossom in each season and grace the air she breathes with the scent of possibility.

Almighty,

Instill in my friend a new way of walking through this life. Let her gait and pace be infused with strength as she walks with confidence through each door that opens and along each path that appears. Give her the courage to make her way in Your way. Protect her as she makes choices and hold her high as she takes leaps of faith.

Dear friend, may god's presence warm you like the sun.

Dear Lord,

It isn't easy to pursue a new endeavor—to find the energy, gather resources, make plans, and put hope in something yet unseen. But as I watch my friend trust You and Your promises, I realize that all those other needs really aren't her burdens to bear. You are providing the way for her, and You will give her exactly what her new journey requires.

Creator of all,

How awesome are the amber walls of the canyon that You formed with the power of the sea. How mysterious and bright are the stars that You drape across the night's sky! Your strength is even evident in the gracefulness of my friend. She is one of my dearest reminders of Your work as an artist. Thank You for the portrait of Your loving attention to detail that You give the world through the inner and outer beauty of my dear friend.

Protector,

My friend's heart has been broken. She guards it now by shying away from her moments to shine. She hides her gifts and strengths because it can be painful to step out on a limb and trust again. God, help her be open and willing to embrace the opportunities You place in front of her. Let her know that You will protect her, so that she can be free to experience Your goodness and power working through her. And when nerves and memories get the best of her, remind her that she is never alone.

amen

Don't judge each day by the harvest you reap, but by the seeds you plant.

ROBERT LOUIS STEVENSON

Psalm 37:7

love and legacy

Dear friend,

Such a heritage is being born of your heart. Your kindness toward anyone you encounter leaves a lasting impression of God's love. I have watched a person's face transform when you speak to them with sincere words of encouragement and hope. It's a beautiful, outward reminder of the graceful changes their heart is experiencing in that moment of acceptance and unconditional love.

Friend, I pray that you have this experience tenfold. When you enter God's presence in prayer and praise, may His words and endless compassion and love for you deepen your roots of faith. May you experience a supernatural supply of mercy as you give time and time again from the well of God's love to friends, family, and everyone God brings into your presence. Your legacy is far reaching…deep and wide. What a gift you are.

I trust in God's unfailing love
for ever and ever.
For what you have done I will always praise you
in the presence of your faithful people.
And I will hope in your name,
for your name is good.

PSALM 52:8-9

God,

Shower my friend with Your richest, most meaningful love experiences: the sense of belonging and being known that comes with family ties, the connection and camaraderie of friends, the beauty and tenderness of romance, and the divine intimacy of being Your child. Weave together these threads of love and let them become a covering and comfort for her life.

Lord,

My friend gives with an open hand and open heart. She never expects anything in return. When she offers her time and resources, she does so without a hint of duty. What a gift this is to each person who is a recipient of her soul's generosity. God, as she comes to You with needs of her own, I pray that each and every one of us who has been blessed by her selflessness will be in tune to Your leading, so that we might be Your hands, Your voice, and a part of Your provision…just when she needs it most.

Dear friend, I celebrate the day you were born because you are a gift to me.

Dear Father,

Your sweet daughter is my friend. I cherish her and place such value on our time together. Thank You for forming such a wonderful person and for giving us both the wisdom to see more than just an acquaintance in the other. When she tilts her head, smiles, and looks at me with curiosity, I know that we are so lucky because, despite our differences, we "get" each other. I take such a miracle as Your handiwork. I am blessed to know Your child and to be known by her.

God,

We can't know how our interactions today will impact another person tomorrow, but, God, with all the ways my friend gives to others, I pray she will have an inkling of the legacy she is leaving. She gives You the credit for every good thing that comes into her life and is quick to give You praise for the opportunity to share with others. Bless her, Lord. I know what she would love above all else...even more ways to share!

LOVE

Jesus,

May Your love flow through my friend's life with such force and truth that she never questions it, searches for a substitution, or doubts her identity as Your adored daughter. May the legacy of Your faithfulness inspire her to always trust Your presence, seek Your will, lift up her needs to You in confidence, and walk in Your ways. I pray that she receives as much encouragement and support from those of us in her life as we do from her sincere, generous offering of love.

 amen

wonder and wisdom

Dear friend,

I hope that you collect many brilliant wonders along your personal pilgrimage through life. May you watch for and notice the very best delights that God is presenting to you each day. String together jewels of truth and adorn your life with them. Pluck a lovely bouquet of good memories and use it as a centerpiece for your times spent with dear ones. Bind together the wisdom of God's Word and keep the volumes in your heart for handy reference. Stand beneath a colorful rainbow and marvel at His promises.

Don't ever forget that God is guiding your steps, nurturing your soul, and clearing your path so that you can delight in His good works and share the bounty of His wisdom with the world.

Trust in the **Lord** and do good;
dwell in the land and enjoy safe pasture.
take delight in the **Lord**
and he will give you the desires of your heart.
PSALM 37:3-4

Dear friend, your thoughtfulness breathes wisdom into my life.

Represent the Lord Himself as close to you and behold how lovingly and humbly He is teaching you. Believe me, you should remain with so good a friend as long as you can. If you grow accustomed to having Him present at your side, and He sees that you do so with love and that you go about striving to please Him; He will never fail you; He will help you in all your trials; you will find Him everywhere.

SAINT TERESA OF AVILA

God,

I ask for Your wonder to fill my friend. I pray that her expanding capacity to see the miraculous and the wonderful becomes her way to understand Your vast, marvelous love. When responsibilities and concerns slow her steps and cloud her thoughts, awaken her to the miraculous and the amusing happenings about her. Release her from the anchors of angst and worry so that her daydreams rise up to meet You like a helium balloon set free at the county fair.

Psalm 5:11

Lord,

Please give my friend splendid moments in the sun. May she shed her shoes and stretch out in a hammock. And if that isn't an option, lead her to the warmth of friendship and the easy sway of conversation with kindred spirits. I pray that Your transforming touch reshapes her days of routine into expansive opportunities for awe and inspiration and that an incredible faith adventure transpires.

Teacher,

My friend has such a genuine eagerness to absorb Your wisdom. Let her walk in Your way so that she can be strengthened in every challenge and every achievement. Give her discernment to know when and how You are moving through her life. Bless her with a heart that hungers to know and reflects the justice, grace, and redemption You teach in every moment that she is Your faithful student.

My Lord,

You know everything about my friend. You know exactly how her struggles and her gifts meld together to shape her strength as she walks in Your wisdom. Connect her to others who feed her faith and who celebrate her unique, amazing presence. May I never hold back from letting her know that I love her and am grateful for her friendship.

Dear friend, as I imagine us sipping iced coffee together at an outdoor café, sunshine brightens my gray day.

god,

I ask You to bless my friend with knowledge that nourishes her soul and life. May she hunger for integrity, peace, compassion, honesty, and a transforming relationship with You. Let there be a gentle leading of truth when false beliefs about herself, You, or life choices enter her thoughts. May the rich truths that are part of Your great plan for her fill her with assurance, energy, and the absolute delight of knowing how wonderful it is to be Your daughter.

amen